Jennie Gorman

REVIEWS:

'Jennie Gorman is one of those rare individuals that you meet once in a lifetime! I am honoured to know such a remarkable woman with the biggest heart and capacity to care and give unconditionally! Jennie has a unique gift which she generously shares in her new book 'Awesome Authenticity', which I read from cover to cover in one sitting and absolutely loved it! If you are seeking to excel in business and build long standing authentic connections, this book is for you! I highly recommend it.'
Josie Thomson
www.josiethomson.com

'As you read this book you can hear Jennie speaking in that warm clear voice which gives you absolute confidence that she is speaking from both her heart and her brain. She is sharing 30 years of learning……..and what Jennie does amazingly well is share her knowledge – it is who she is.
This book is easy to read and digest. It makes you sit back, reflect and move forward with your life. I recommend this book!'
Aaron Goldwater
www.juratsoftware.com

'I have just finished reading Jennie Gorman's book 'Awesome Authenticity' ! WOW! What a read! The knowledge that Jennie shares in her book is GOLD! This book is a MUST read for all people who are in business....'
Stacey Huish
www.only-effective-communication-skills.com

*'Jennie Gorman is nothing short of an exemplary human being, and has a fantastic reputation amongst business leaders in Australia. Whenever I mention Jennie to a business person I know (it seems like everyone knows her), they always rave about her. That's because she's an absolute master of creating and nurturing authentic relationships. Awesome Authenticity is a must have business book. It is an inspirational, thought **provoking**, step by step guide filled with nuggets of wisdom that every business owner must know in order to achieve joy and success simultaneously in business and in life. I have no doubt that if you read 'Awesome Authenticity', complete the simple yet eye opening self- assessments, and follow Jennie's advice that you will catapult to greater success in more ways than you can imagine.'*
Natasha Howie
www.ascendmedia.com.au

I have known the awesome Jennie Gorman for many years and I know of her excellent people skills. I was eager to read her book 'Awesome Authenticity'. When I started reading the book I couldn't put it down. It was so exciting to read on every page the enormously useful hints and tips to promote relationships and business opportunities. Jennie is a rare gem in this busy world of entrepreneurs and business people trying to gain some recognition. She shares her knowledge and experience on every page. Everyone can gain invaluable knowledge and expertise by reading her book. I was very inspired by reading 'Awesome Authenticity' and I can highly recommend it to anyone who seeks to build relationships. Jennie you are awesome.

Tove Vine,
http://www.tovevine.com

AWESOME
Authenticity

JENNIE GORMAN

Awesome Authenticity
© Jennie Gorman 2015
1st Edition August 2013
2nd Edition July 2014

All rights reserved. No part of this publication may be reproduced, stored in a retrieval system, or transmitted in any form or by any means, electronic, mechanical, photocopying, recording or otherwise, without the prior written permission of the author.

National Library of Australia Cataloguing-in-Publication entry (pbk)

Creator:	Gorman, Jennie, author.
Title:	Awesome Authenticity : mastering business relationships
Edition:	3rd edition
ISBN:	978-0-9943041-5-5 (paperback)
Subjects:	Business people. Interpersonal relations. Business networks. Business communication.
Dewey Number:	650.13

Published by Percy Cooper and InHouse Publishing
www.inhousepublishing.com.au

Printed using Envirocare paper.

DEDICATION

I dedicate this book to those entrepreneurs courageous or crazy enough to be in business for themselves. To my clients and friends who have walked with me on my path over the last 20+ years, who have supported my learning and gained from my teachings, I say

THANK YOU!

At any one time there are more than 2 million people in Australia running their own small business, and an additional half a million working on getting a start-up off the ground.

Unfortunately, by 2017 almost 40% of the established businesses trading today will more than likely be out of business, and more than 50% of new businesses entering the market in 2013 will have bitten the dust.

CONTENTS

Reviews: i
Dedication vii
Acknowledgements 1
1   Being totally authentic 3
2   Why relationship building is my life 9
3   Do you know your why? 15
4   How to build your business via word of mouth 21
5   How to build your business relationships?
    A self-assessment 29
6   The basics in building lasting relationships 37
7   Do you wonder why you are networking? 43
8   Networking successfully equals listening 47
9   Relationship building for success 51
10 Do you leave networking to chance? 55
11 My success formula for events 61
12 Twelve traits that make a networker outstanding 67
13 Prospecting Vs Networking 75
14 Ten tips for start-up businesses 79
15 The difference between
    networking and netweaving 85
16 A referral network that gives you leads 93
17 How to make your business grow in the future............ 97

18	Making a positive difference is easier than you think.. 103
19	Be more than good, be awesome 109
20	Customer service the best add-on you can give........... 115
21	Relationship marketing can take you to the next level... 121
22	Why resilience is important in relationship building 127
23	Networking vs. Masterminding....................................... 133
24	The ultimate tool for business success........................... 139
25	Why is masterminding so powerful?.............................. 143
26	Want to move your business forward?........................... 149
27	Benefits of masterminding... 155
28	Accountability in business.. 161
29	Get your own board of directors..................................... 167
30	Million dollar lasting relationships 171
31	How to set your goals and make them a reality 177
32	Don't ask yourself what the world needs....................... 183
33	The power of vision... 187
34	Awesome abundance... 193
	About the author 199

ACKNOWLEDGEMENTS

I wonder how it is possible to acknowledge all the people who have supported me during the journey of these three editions. There are so many people to thank especially the following:

A very special thank you to all my friends and clients who have supported me at **Connexions Unlimited** over the years;

to **Margaret Wilmink,** who has been there as a wonderful friend as well as my 'Meeter and Greeter' at my events;

to all my **MasterMinders** who have supported me in my growth and creation of something that for me has been a work of art;

to **Tam Ho** and **Tanja Caprioli** thank you for being there as MasterMind co-facilitators;

to **Bet Millear, Peter Gorman** and **Margaret Wilmink** thank you for the tireless job of proofreading;

AWESOME AUTHENTICITY

to **Josie Thomson, Natasha Howie, Tove Vine, Stacey Huish** and **Aaron Goldwater** THANKYOU for your reviews added into this book;

to **Stu Fisher**, thank you for your loving support and overwhelming belief in me and this book;

to my daughter **Rachael Lowing** and my son **Nigel Gorman:** thank you for being who you are. I am proud to be your mother and grandmother to your children;

and of course, without whom this book would not have come into a third edition, thank you to **Ocean Reeve** from **InHouse Publishing**.

1
BEING TOTALLY AUTHENTIC

AWESOME AUTHENTICITY

I hear you asking, what does she mean by being **'totally authentic'** and having **'awesome authenticity'**? To be awesome is to be awe-inspiring and by being authentic in all you say and do, changes the way you are seen by others. It is important in today's business world to be seen for who you really are, by being believable, trusted and sometimes vulnerable. I believe that there is no difference between who you are in business or in your personal life. The basics of 'who you are' needs to resonate in both.

In business today we need to be awe-inspiringly real … it is about being yourself and knowing your own self-worth. No-one really ever wants you to be someone other than who you really are.

Awesomeness comes from deep inside you, and for many people they are not even aware of their own awesomeness. We all have it and need to acknowledge it and allow the door to open to honesty by setting ourselves free so we can become truly authentic.

To be authentic is to be truly REAL and be who you WANT to be, not who you think you need to become. It is not about anyone else, it is about YOU.

Your truth is what you project in every thought, word, feeling and action. Authenticity equals truth, the truth that you feel in every fibre of your being. It comes from your heart not your head. When you feel it, it resonates in you a good feeling. By understanding your own true and authentic self, you will find who you really are. Allow others to see and know you ... reveal yourself, for you are unique and special.

We all have within us hidden fears, doubts and worries. It is important to allow the wise and powerful part of ourselves, often called 'the higher self,' the opportunity to show itself. We need to let our unique passion, values, visions, talents, abilities and our sense of purpose, be seen.

Until you really understand your real purpose of why you are here and what you are to do in this life, you will be short-changing yourself by not showing the world your true unique identity. When you understand what you are here in this life to do and be, then you will know the importance of leaving a legacy behind you, when your time on earth is over. I often say to my clients, what do you want people to say about you when you die and your name is mentioned?

What is the dash (-) between a birth and death date? Did the person make their mark? Were they memorable for the good work they did? So, for you, are you making the most of the time between your birth and yet to come death? It is the 'dash' that people will remember.

As we gain conscious awareness, we learn how to live a life of joy, peace, love, freedom, abundance, gratitude and all the other beautiful things life allows us to be, while being in tune with who we really are every moment of our day, every day.

I am not saying there won't be worry and stress in your life. This is necessary for you to develop and become who you are. We only learn through experiences we have so it's necessary to be pushed at times, sometimes further than we want.

So, open the door and become who you really are by setting yourself free to be REAL! Become a master of your life and live purposefully.

AWESOME AUTHENTICITY

2
WHY RELATIONSHIP BUILDING IS MY LIFE

Building relationships is the same for both personal and business

- Jennie Gorman

AWESOME AUTHENTICITY

Building relationships for me has been a part of my life for as long as I can remember. It is my passion and my belief that we need to help and support everyone to understand what they have to offer others so they too can live on purpose and have a fulfilled life.

Relationship building in the business world is often called **networking**. When I first started consciously **business networking** the word '**networking**' was used to identify computer peripherals.

From a child through to the late 1980s I was not aware that I was **networking,** as people and how their minds ticked, always fascinated me. I was doing what was shown me by my parents. I think I must have been a 'WHY' child who asked too many questions. I was fascinated why people thought the way they did. My father told me that as a small child I spent my time dancing, singing and laughing. No wonder these things still mean so much to me now, not that I dance much physically, but in my head I still do and rhythm is in my blood.

I was lucky and blessed to be born with this curiosity. My parents, and going back for many generations, have proved this by the things that they did with their lives.

I am told seven generations creates the patterns in our cellular memory, and as I love genealogy, I have been fortunate enough to trace that far back and recognise the attributes of my ancestors. My family were always **givers** rather than takers, so it was natural for me to be like that and to teach that to my children. I believe I was blessed to have good role models from day one.

I discovered over 25 years ago that there was a way to create better **relationships** in what people call **networking, word-of-mouth marketing or relationship building**. I soon realised, as no-one at that time was writing about it, or I hadn't come across any books, that there was a system of what is now talked about as **giver's gain, appreciation marketing, go-giving** or **referral marketing.** It is all the same theme no matter what you call it.

To be the **'go-giver'** you have to be prepared to give to others first, without expectation of something in return. When we are **giving**, there is always a **receiver**, so we have to be open to both these processes for it to really work and make a difference in other's lives.

In the very early 1990's I became aware of 'my' process of relationship building which I still use today.

I began to write about it and then teach it. I wanted people to learn the significance of what I called **networking basics** and how important it is to become a professional networker, if you want to develop your business. It really is a very simple attitude change for most people. Unfortunately, we live in a society that wants to know WIIFM (what's in it for me?), rather than, 'what can I do for you?'

Appreciation marketing is so very easy to do! Show people you meet that you appreciate them. Everyone likes to feel special. Gratitude for who you are, what you have, who you know and where you are now, is what sets you apart.

Networking is such a buzz word these days and people continue to go to events on a regular basis in the hope of gaining more business and meeting more people.

Why, I ask? Most times they have no idea why they are there, what they are meant to be doing, and what they are going to do after the event. I believe that by not having **goals** for your **business networking** you are wasting your time, money and energy. All of which are precious today and not always as easy to come by as in the past. People say to me, 'I gave someone my card and they never contacted me.' I ask, 'Why would they? Who are you to them?'

Relationship building is not something that happens overnight. It takes time, sometimes years, to develop a relationship that will move through, what I call the loyalty ladder, to becoming a referral. I believe that there are seven steps up the ladder.

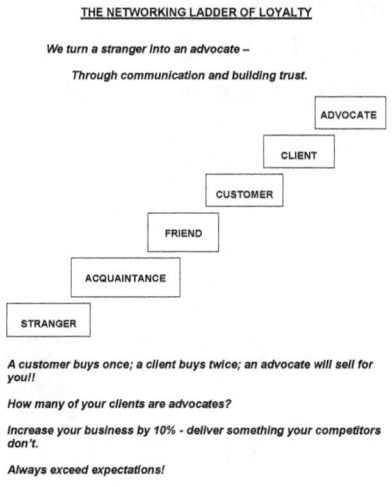

THE NETWORKING LADDER OF LOYALTY

We turn a stranger into an advocate – Through communication and building trust.

A customer buys once; a client buys twice; an advocate will sell for you!!

How many of your clients are advocates?

Increase your business by 10% - deliver something your competitors don't.

Always exceed expectations!

Are you worthy of someone's **referral**? I really believe that 'people buy people' firstly, not your product or service. Have you created a good enough bond, knowledge or impression that they would want to buy or link with you?

When **referring** someone or a business it must be genuine, solid and come up with whatever is necessary to fulfil the want of the person wanting the 'product/service'. You will be judged on the type of referrals you give, so don't become known for 'bad referrals'.

Trust and **integrity** are the two words that come to mind that are important if you wish to have a strong **relationship** with someone.

As a referrer, it is '**who you know**' and '**who knows you**' that makes the difference. So, what sort of a **networker** are you?

Are you a good referrer? Do you have good solid relationships? Are you trusted in the marketplace?

I suggest you ask people around you if this is how they see you and if not, change the attitude!

For me, my business and personal contacts are of utmost importance. I see them as one. I am happy to help and support anyone when people value what I have to give.

3
DO YOU KNOW YOUR WHY?

AWESOME AUTHENTICITY

This I believe is one of the most important questions one needs to answer themselves; about their own life initially and particularly when they start a business.

If you do not know or understand your **WHY** for being in business, you more than likely are not doing your passion and your 'real' work. If you do not feel the passion in your life, why are you living and what makes your heart sing?

Knowing your **'WHY'** is one of the hardest questions for most new business owners to answer. I find in my **Business MasterMind Groups** that most people who have been in business for some time still can't answer this question. I believe that if you do not understand the 'why' of your business and your life, what you want and what legacy you can leave behind, then your 'why' is not big enough to sustain you and your business in the long run.

Being in business today is hard for solo and small business entrepreneurs and most often, they have to do nearly everything themselves. More often than not, it is one person working hard to do the roles of up to 8 people.

We all have our own innate gifts. These are the things we do without thinking and wonder at times why we get paid to do them, as they are so easy for us. It is the other parts of business we have to do that aren't easy where we struggle. These things have to be done and that takes us out of our own flow.

For me, one of the most difficult parts of my business to contend with is the accounting side, which of course is the most important part if I want to get paid! I now understand that this is not one of my innate gifts so I need a good bookkeeper and an accountant to look after these things for me, explaining what I need to know and understand if my business is to be successful.

When you understand the importance of doing what is easy for you, you will then see why outsourcing in business can change your world. This allows you the time to work on your business using your innate gifts by presenting them to the world.

So, getting back to your 'why'. I believe if your 'why' makes you cry, you know you are doing what you need to be doing. That is, living on purpose.

When I talk about my 'why', I can't help the emotion that comes up within me, because for me it is my overwhelming passion and reason for being alive.

I want to share this with others to give them the opportunities to achieve what they want to achieve in life. If what they think is their 'why' and they are not in their flow, we then know they are not doing their purpose. We are all born with something special to do. Often it is our hobby initially, until one day we realise that we have a special something that we can share with others.

Whatever that is, and if it is all-consuming, you will most likely find that this is the **WHY** that you have been blessed to have and to share. Once you understand this, everything will change in your life.

Only you can know what this is. It is something that you need to sit with, meditate on, think and or write about. We are all different and can use different methods to achieve what we want to achieve by trying one of these or similar. By being aware of your thoughts, where your consciousness is and feeling what you feel, you will come up with the answers when you are ready.

I often ask my clients the following questions to find out if they have or are aware of their 'why'. I ask you to ponder on these questions when you have time, so as to gain more clarity of who you are and why you are doing what you are doing ….

Do you know what your gifts are?

What is your cause and belief?

What inspires you to be who you are?

Does it bring tears to your eyes?

What brings up an overwhelming feeling in your heart that almost chokes you at times?

By understanding and answering these questions, you will ultimately know if what you are doing really is your purpose in this life.

Being **REAL** in business is what having **authentic business relationships** is all about. This will support you to understand your reason and mission in life and then you can create this and be truly happy.

AWESOME AUTHENTICITY

4
HOW TO BUILD YOUR BUSINESS VIA WORD OF MOUTH

The most stabilising force behind any business, I believe, is through **'word of mouth'**, **'networking'** or **'business relationship building.'** I personally prefer to use the words 'word of mouth' or 'business relationship building,' as people around the world often relate the word networking to multi-level/internet marketing or interconnected computer peripherals.

Not only do we need friends and supporters in our personal lives, we also need them in business. There are several reasons for this, and several types of relationships that need to be built if we are going to be successful.

Making money isn't always the reason for some people. Personally, it is not my main reason for what I do. Of course I need to earn money to live and survive. I do accept for many, though, that this is their number one priority. I then would ask the question, why? Maybe it is for a lifestyle so you can then eventually do your purpose?

This is an individual question and can't be answered by anyone else when it comes to understanding 'your why'.

If you are currently in your own business, especially as a solo business owner, you know the going can get tough.

It's the community and relationships you build around you that can make the difference between keeping your doors open or having to close them.

Another primary reason for relationship building is mutual support and contribution through the education and guidance you both give and receive. Every person you meet has something to teach or give you. Likewise, you have something to teach or give them.

Sometimes it can be a good idea to get clarity about where you are in your business relationships by making a list. This will be of people that help, edify, teach, refer or otherwise support you to grow you and your business.

Who are the people who believe in you and are willing to tell you the truth even when you may not want to hear it? These are your business friends and maybe, your independent board of directors.

These people are a very important foundation for your business, especially if you are in small business. Personal friends and family not involved in your business will often tend to be negative as they try to protect you from what they perceive as failure in the future.

Do not listen to them as they will only sabotage you from doing what you need to do.

Listen to your business friends who know your work and what you stand for in the business world.

People used to refer to the 'old boys network', who as a group of mates, usually men, referred their buddies for future business. There is a difference in the marketplace today though.

Where once people referred friends and colleagues without considering the effectiveness of these contacts, I now believe people work more on the level of 'trust' rather than just the 'like'.

A referral is a reflection of you in the marketplace so make sure you give one that will be successful in some way, if followed up properly. You and your reputation will be affected if the referral you give is not a good one!

The most important thing in any business is your attitude and the extent of your daily communication skills.

This will show how you maintain your integrity and reputation.

Consider your business communications as a stepping stone to not only the person you are communicating with but also the people they know as well. **Word of mouth** is a powerful tool to harness.

Referral is the easiest way to build a good and solid foundation for any business, and the repeat business that comes from it, strengthens it. It is far easier and more cost effective to keep an existing client than look for a new one!

Nurture the opportunities that come your way by providing something of value. It never hurts to be the first person to put something on the table. It builds trust in a world where trust is often challenged. While you do need to look after your cash flow, it can be a good idea to sometimes consider opportunities that won't make you money, because sometimes these opportunities build dynamic pathways to larger financial avenues.

A good example of this is the female publicist who began working with an unknown author because she had faith in his abilities.

As it turned out, this author was a fountain of contacts within not only the media industry but to other well-known authors and world renowned businesses.

The work performed by the publicist free of charge, for this one person, became the best advertising ever generated for her business. In turn the relationship she built with the author became bonded for life through goodwill.

Let's consider the possibilities for you to find and build more business relationships. What organisations do you belong to, discussion lists, open forums, breakfast networks, social media groups etc.? I've heard too often from business owners that they do not have time to join groups and 'socialise.' Believe me, you don't have the luxury not to, especially if you have a small business. It's not only necessary … it's vital.

The top CEOs and salespeople around the world know that the golf course is the best and most successful way to build a solid relationship with the people they are searching out. So, find the interest of the person you wish to get to know, and combine that with your meetings. You may be surprised at how successful this can be, as well as a lot of fun during the process.

Social media gives you the opportunities to start the relationship and face-to-face gives you the opportunity to cement it!

This brings me to one of the most important business-building tools necessary from my perspective. It is your business card. **This is your shop window**. It may be the one thing that makes someone contact you in the future.

I am surprised though at the number of people I meet who don't have a card at all, or who have a professional business card with incorrect information. Your card must give all your contact details as well as information of what you do and what services you offer. I also recommend that solos and SMEs, if possible, have their photograph on their card. This cements the connection with the card owner and the person receiving the card.

Another way to support your business is to find someone whom you trust to give the same professionalism and service as yourself, in a complementary business. You can then support each other in what we call co-operative business building. This is very effective and time saving. Collaboration or joint venturing can leverage you and your business to that next level.

If you haven't already started to build your network, it's time to locate the organisations in your industry and start making friends. It will pay you back one hundred fold. Building relationships in business, is in effect, building your business, so consider it time well spent and get started today!

AWESOME AUTHENTICITY

5
HOW TO BUILD YOUR BUSINESS RELATIONSHIPS A SELF-ASSESSMENT

Business networking will help you build your profile
- Jennie Gorman

AWESOME AUTHENTICITY

The first thing to understand about building successful relationships using the word-of-mouth method is how you do it now, and how you would like to do it better in the future.

Are you successful now as a networker?

Would you like to become more effective in your word-of-mouth marketing?

By doing this self-analysis you will discover for yourself how effective you are at this present time and how you can become more successful in the future. This is a guide for you to follow and will show you your effectiveness in the marketplace at this moment.

REMEMBER, this is not for self-criticism. It is to support you to become a better networker. Understanding how you network now may not be as effective as you would like and below will give you some new ideas.

1. Have you written clear and well-defined goals for your present networking activities?

Yes   No

2. Do you have a scheduled plan of action for your networking?

Yes   No

3. At social or business functions, do you go with a commitment to leave with the names of 1 or 2 new people who YOU may be able to support to meet THEIR personal and professional goals?

      Always   Sometimes   Never

4. At social or business functions, do you go with a commitment to leave with the names of at least 1 or 2 new people who may be able to support YOU to meet YOUR personal and professional goals?

      Always   Sometimes   Never

5. Do you make a point of following up quickly and appropriately with those people with whom you have just 'connected'?

      Always   Sometimes   Never

6. Do you keep an organised and accessible file of information on people you have met including interests, occupations, hobbies, conversations, birthday etc.? This is very important if your memory isn't good.

      Yes   No

7.   Do you make it a point to schedule a specific time every week to 're-connect' with people you've met but haven't spoken with for a while?

        Yes   Sometimes   No

8.   Do you check the internet, emails, newspapers and/or magazines weekly to seek out interesting activities and opportunities that might help you meet your personal and career goals?

        Always   Sometimes   Never

9.   Have you set aside 'specific' before/after work and/or lunch times each week to confer with people who can help you and your career goals?

        Always   Sometimes   Never

10.   Have you met with a new networking acquaintance in the past fortnight?

        Yes   No

11. Are you connected to LinkedIn, Facebook, Twitter, Google+, Pinterest and other social media marketing organisations known as SMM?

        Yes   No

12. Do you have at least one Business Page connected to Facebook?

        Yes   No

13. Have you created a Business Page on Google+?

        Yes   No

14. Have you created a Business Page on LinkedIn?
        Yes   No

15. Do you have a business card that's easy to read, has your photo on it and gives all your correct information?
    Yes   Nearly All   No

16. Have you considered going to the next step from Networking to Masterminding?

        Yes   No

On completion add your score:
10 points = "YES" answer,
5 points = "SOMETIMES/NEARLY ALL",
0 points = "NEVER" or "NO".

Your score shows you where you are now as a networker only and is not a reflection of you or how you can become better. Please use this knowledge as a support for your networking growth.

AWESOME AUTHENTICITY

6
THE BASICS IN BUILDING LASTING RELATIONSHIPS

Integrity in business is not optional it is essential

- Jennie Gorman

AWESOME AUTHENTICITY

Building relationships with people that will last, creating win-win connections and who will become your 'raving fans' are all based on a few simples rules.

Firstly, you need to establish **trust**.

I ask you, do you trust yourself and your ability to make good judgements? Trust is all about knowing yourself and how authentic you come across to people meeting you for the first time. Do you give the feeling to others that you are someone who can be relied upon and can keep their word? Do you have faith and belief in others? Can you be relied upon to do the right thing?

These are all questions one needs to ask oneself when looking at the basics in relationship building. By trusting someone it does not necessarily mean that that person is trustworthy. Being too trusting without thinking about it carefully can sometimes be dangerous. There are people who gain trust and then break it, so you need to use discretion on where you give your trust.

I believe that building your **credibility** is the next thing to look at when creating solid relationships. Credibility is how your words and deeds are seen by others.

Are you trustworthy and do you have expertise on the subject you are talking about? To gain credibility in the business world, you need to prove it firstly by the way you act, as well as knowing that the information you pass on is correct and reliable. People will view you by the company you keep and what is perceived as your established reliability.

How you treat others is a reflection on you as a person. It has been said that 'you should treat others as you would like to be treated'. I personally disagree with this statement. I believe that we 'should treat others as **they would like to be treated**'.

This is far better from my perspective, as the first way is assuming that the person has the same values as you yourself. The way I would like to be treated would be very different from many other people. Take, for example, the giving of a gift. How many times have you been given a gift by someone who gives what they like and is their taste, but quite contrary to your own? It is very easy to assume what others like. The only way to truly know what someone likes is to listen to what they say, watch how they live and observe how they do things.

I believe that making a habit of **acknowledging people** is a wonderful attribute to have. Making others feel good and worthwhile helps create a relationship.

We are not aware, I believe, of what is going on in another's life. Praise or kindness can change a person's world dramatically if they are someone who does not get enough of this in their life. It must be sincere though and come 'from the heart'.

Observing people and acknowledging what they are doing or have created can be very powerful. It is important that we create win-win situations in all our relationships.

To remember important dates and significant events in another's life can show your awareness of them. Isn't it nice to be remembered on your birthday or anniversary, or if your work mates and friends acknowledge something you have done well?

We are sometimes very aware of what is not necessary to remember, and all too often forget the significant times in people's lives. Bringing joy and happiness to another's life can be very easy and simple.

Like a smile, it is free!

If you want to create solid lasting relationships, be prepared to **invest time** and energy into that relationship. Take the first step … don't wait for someone else to take that first action.

Relationships that last and are productive for both sides are worth the time and energy that one needs to put into them.

So remember these attributes: trust, credibility, how you treat and acknowledge others, investing time and energy while never forgetting important dates and events. These are all the basic ingredients to building relationships that last forever.

AWESOME AUTHENTICITY

7
DO YOU WONDER WHY YOU ARE NETWORKING?

Choose wisely what you want because it will become a reality

— Jennie Gorman

AWESOME AUTHENTICITY

This is a question I ask people quite often. I believe, if you are not aware of why you network, your outcome will not be what you are hoping and wishing to achieve.

Is your reason to become a better networker one of these:
- career building
- developing a higher profile
- earning more money - financial gain or
- to gain influence in your community or business network?

This is an important question. If you understand why you are networking, you will find that you will have a clearer vision of what you want.

By not understanding this and what you expect to gain, you will not move forward. Word-of-mouth marketing has been around forever and is a powerful way to build your business.

I believe, done correctly, it is the best way to build the relationships and business you want for the future. I have proved it over many years.

If for you, networking becomes a natural way of life, it becomes the most successful way to do business. It is necessary for you to learn the basics if you wish to be successful though. It is all about relationship building.

You will find that after a while you don't even think about what you are doing. Networking should always be a win-win for all parties, so always repay appropriately favours extended to you.

Remember, when you give a referral, notify the receiver and the person who is being referred. This way they are both on the same page. I find emailing or texting the easiest and quickest way to do this.

It is important to give information as to why you are referring the person so that both are aware of what has been passed on. This helps both sides to have more of an idea of the relationship with the referrer. Always make it clear what your relationship is with the person you are referring.

For example, are they a client, a personal friend, someone you feel that they could have a good synergy with, or you have or haven't done business with them, etc.

Another important thing to remember is that you need to be seen, become known and move into the market place appropriate to you, at your own pace, always keeping in mind why you are doing it. Attend one or two specific networking groups and become known as a 'regular'. People then perceive you as stable, reliable and trustworthy and will then do business with you.

It is important you find your niche market, so the types of events you attend must be appropriate for your needs.

How many networking groups you go to is up to you but I do suggest initially that you limit it to no more than 2 a week otherwise you do not have time to follow up and meet if appropriate. Also, remember that you do need to work both 'on' and 'in' your business as well.

Remember, that the people you are looking to do business with, are looking for you too!

8
NETWORKING SUCCESSFULLY EQUALS LISTENING

Listening is the most important part of networking

— Jennie Gorman

One of the most important parts of networking and building relationships is **listening**. This is a skill that successful and professional sales people use to perfection.

Are you really hearing what the speaker is saying? Are you watching them as well?

Listening is more than listening with your ears to someone's voice and the words they are saying. It is all about watching their expressions as well as their movements and gestures. Look at the eyes of the person whom you are speaking with, be involved and listen to what isn't being said too! This will help with your questioning.

To be successful as a networker you need to be a great listener as well as being alert and interested in what the speaker is saying.

Body language can tell you more than the words that are said.

Really listening to what the person is saying, what their needs are and where you can support them, will bring you clients and advocates quicker than anything else. When you are speaking with a prospective client, find out what they are really wanting and needing.

Can you support them with something totally unrelated to their or your work? Can you pass on a good referral from your contacts that may be able to help them achieve what they are wishing to achieve?

AWESOME AUTHENTICITY

I have said for many years that we have been given two eyes and one mouth … so use the eyes before the mouth. If you allow the person you are communicating with to talk at least twice as much as you do, then you will learn things that you would not have naturally learnt by doing all the talking. Only ask questions that are pertaining to them.

The greatest compliment you can give someone is to listen to them, as people naturally love to talk, especially about themselves or their products. Really listen though and ask questions as much as you can. This way you are empowering and encouraging them to tell you more.

It is important if the conversation bores you that you do not show it or get a glazed-over look in your eyes. There is nothing worse than being a bystander and observing this. **A bored listener shows too!**

If you feel that this is happening when you are speaking with someone, you need to move away from the conversation as quickly as possible or change the subject that is being discussed. Others around you will notice your lack of interest and usually, it is not the person who is doing all the talking.

So, start listening more and finding out some interesting information that can support your clients as well when you are in conversation. If you are able to refer someone to your friends, customers and clients, it is a great way to let them know that you are supporting them.

"I never learn anything talking. I only learn things when I ask questions." - Lou Holtz

9
RELATIONSHIP BUILDING FOR SUCCESS

I have realised that people generally "don't know, what they don't know". Have you found that in what you do too?

We all think that we know about a subject or industry until we actually take the time to learn about the subject ourself, and I know that it is quite often never what I thought it was!

I have found that this is very true when it comes to **networking**.

People generally think that they know what they are doing and why they are at an event, without really understanding what good networking practices are all about.

So, consequently, they don't get the results they were looking to gain.

I believe there is a formula that will support anyone wishing to use word of mouth marketing to take their business to success.

It appears that one of the main reasons for most people networking is to gain 'referrals', but to do this, we need to develop good relationships first. This doesn't happen without you taking some action.

What actions do you take in your networking? Do you know who you are looking to meet and who your prospective clients actually are? We need to know and understand our niche market so that we know where and when to network.

Networking is not just about attending events and hoping that something magic will happen in your business because you gave people your business card. It is about creating relationships with the people you meet and liked and maybe whose business and yours have some synergy. You need to take action by making the first move, because if you wait for them, it won't happen!

As mentioned previously, I ask people to consider firstly WHY they are networking, as it is the 'why' that helps you understand what you need to do. Different 'whys' mean you will network differently. When you understand your 'why', you need to consider what and where your niche market is and then look for the type of events that will support you to meet the people who will help you to achieve your outcomes.

Once you know the reasons 'why you are networking', 'where the best places are', 'what your target market is' and 'who you want to meet', you will find only then that are you ready to start the next phase. Initially you need to learn the 'HOW TO' skills to achieving the outcomes and advocates you wish to find.

Your **'raving fans'** are the people who will support you to achieve what you want from your business.

10
DO YOU LEAVE NETWORKING TO CHANCE?

Working in the correct niche will make you achieve faster

— Jennie Gorman

AWESOME AUTHENTICITY

Doors often will open where you thought there would not be a door; and where there wouldn't be a door for anyone else.

As a business person, I know you know that **networking** is important for the **growth** of your business. So, it is necessary to ask yourself the question: **Is YOUR networking building YOUR business**?

We never know where a door will open, do we? Every new meeting is just like this. It may open a door straight away, or maybe that person knows someone who needs your services or could help you. Or maybe, you could help them achieve their outcomes.

Many people who attend **networking events** enjoy the experience but don't attract more clients or increase their business profits. They often don't even build a new relationship from the experience!

Don't expect because someone likes what you do, that they will be keen to catch up for coffee or for more information. They may exchange business cards with you BUT if nothing comes of it, this is NOT their fault!

If this happens to you, consider what you did or didn't do to make this a reality. Why wait for the other person? If you liked them and thought you had synergy make the contact yourself. Do this within the first 24 hours of your meeting.

It is necessary that you be pro-active. Make contact if you liked them and felt they were someone you would like to know for you and or your clients in the future.

If you want to have a good relationship with someone, you need to put in too! Maybe the other person is unaware of how to follow up and what is necessary after an event.

It is important to become aware of why you went to the event in the first place and what the outcome was that you wanted. If you do not know why you were there, I suggest you ask yourself these questions:

- Did you have a plan and a goal prior to going?
- What did you do at the event?
- What follow up did you do afterwards?
- Did you stay with people you know because it was hard to get out of your comfort zone?
- Did you introduce yourself to someone you didn't know?
- Did you introduce someone else to someone they didn't know?

If you want to **turn your networking into profits** you need to create relationships with the right people.

They may not even be aware of the potential of knowing you.

Most people don't do business after a first time meeting unless it is a service or product they needed there and then. If you exchanged business cards, I suggest you make contact as soon as possible via email, social media or a phone call. This lets them know that you felt a connection with them initially. You can then follow them up to arrange to get together to learn more about what help they may require for their business!

If you want to form a genuine relationship, you firstly need to put in.

Listen to what they need and then see if you can help them get it! **Remember, networking is not about you all the time!**

Take your networking from ordinary to extraordinary. Not only is **networking an essential life skill**, it is also the most basic **business building** tool in today's competitive market.

Networking accounts for more than 87 per cent of all business in the market place today.

So, how effective a networker are you?
and/or
Do you leave your networking to chance?

AWESOME AUTHENTICITY

11
MY SUCCESS FORMULA FOR EVENTS

Business cards and a good database are the most important tools
— Jennie Gorman

AWESOME AUTHENTICITY

The most obvious thing I notice as a networker when going to networking events is that most event goers are not aware of **how** they can make networking work successfully for themselves and their business.

I believe that there are **four things** you need to do and understand before networking will reach your expectations.

They are knowing **YOUR what, where, why and who** your niche market is, as mentioned previously.

1. **What** are you looking to achieve when you go to events?
2. **Why** do you want to be in that marketplace?
3. Do you know **where** you need to be to meet those business people?
4. Are you aware of **who** you are needing to meet for your future success?

These are really crucial questions if you want to get your networking right. Once you are aware of these four questions you can then set out to achieve what you want in the most cost and time effective way.

Word of mouth marketing is not a 'hit and miss' experience.

I believe that you will have success once you know your niche marketplace and move to that area for your connections.

Prior to going to any event you need to have set **goals** of what you wish to achieve during the time you are there.

Are you setting goals and making sure that they come to fruition? It is important that you accomplish what you set out to do and do not leave the event until you have achieved it.

Socialising is very important and you are there to meet new people, so don't spend too much time with people you know and have developed a relationship with already. Your contact with the people you know needs to be limited to at least a third of your time at the event.

Be aware of people who appear not to know anyone and help them to meet others. This will help you move into new circles of attendees too. Do not leave the event until you have achieved what you went there to do. Don't be pushy in regard to your business, as you are there to learn about the other attendees first!

The most important part of any event is what you do **after you leave** and go back to your office. Make sure you email people you have met that you would like to know better and see again. It is very important that you send a nice friendly email **WITHOUT any promotion** of your business.

One of the **first turn offs** is when someone emails to say 'nice to meet you and here is what I do'. That type of email gives you the license to hit the delete button!

Networking is all about relationship building and giving without expectation of return.

Your first priority is to learn as much as you can about the person you are making contact with, asking them for more and deciding if you wish to meet them again on a one-on-one basis or at a future event.

It is important that the email or message you send states what your intentions are in regards to contacting or meeting up with them in the future. Remember, you do not know who they know. You may be looking for someone for your network who they may know, so it pays to listen to what they are saying while asking questions. Or, you may just want to know them better and develop a relationship with them for the future.

We all have different reasons for our networking and it is very easy to just turn up and expect things to happen. Networking is all about the **ACTION** you take to make it worthwhile for you and your businesses future.

AWESOME AUTHENTICITY

12
TWELVE TRAITS THAT MAKE A NETWORKER OUTSTANDING

Treat others as they would like to be treated

— Jennie Gorman

AWESOME AUTHENTICITY

People often ask 'what are the traits of a good networker'?

Here are 12 traits that I feel make a good networker stand out ... of course, there are more than these 12, but these are probably some of the major ones.

So, do you see yourself as a good or outstanding networker or would you like to become one? All people who have been networking for a long time will tell you that you never stop learning, especially as the marketplace is continually changing and of course people's priorities change with it.

Did you know that great networkers can help you achieve what you want to achieve? They can also take you where you want to go by introducing you to the right people. They hone their skills continuously and you will see them in the marketplace in different venues, with different people and making new connections to help their clients and community.

You may wonder 'What traits does a great networker have to have to help their tribe/community to move to the next level and make them truly outstanding at what they do?'

Here is my list and a little detail of some of the qualities that make a networker stand out:

1. A good networker will **listen and watch** what others are doing – observing while listening to

conversations gives any good networker the opportunity to recognise where and when they can help other people. They think on their feet knowing the best and most appropriate person to help or support the person speaking.

2. A good networker **becomes known** by attending other networkers events – you will notice that a good networker will always support other networkers to build their tribe/community. They will always offer to help out by jumping in without being asked and helping as best they can. A good networker knows no scarcity and is willing to share their contacts, their knowledge and their support. A good networker will always attend other networkers events as often as they can to show their support to 'the cause'.

3. A good networker **follows up** – after meeting someone new or attending an event a good networker will follow up with the people they wish to keep in contact with in the future. They will not judge anyone on who they are and what they do, as they are aware that 'people know people' and you never know who they are. A good referral often comes from an unexpected contact.

4. A good networker **supports and encourages** in public – few things can boost your friends and clients more than praise or testimonials from a peer, especially a peer you look up to. Outstanding networkers recognise the skills of others vocally,

understanding that in group settings the impact of their words is even greater.

5. A good networker **gives good referrals** without expectation – so, become known for giving referrals that are good. You only need to give a bad one for people to comment, so think clearly about who you pass a referral on to. Making sure that there is compatibility between the two people is of upmost importance.

6. A good networker knows and **understands niche marketing** – one of the first things a business needs to understand is who they wish to sell their products and/or services to. For most businesses this is hard to define and break down into their particular niche. I suggest that you try out different niches until you finally settle into a place that is comfortable. It is okay to have more than one niche as long as you keep it separated in your marketing so as not to confuse your clients.

7. A good networker knows and uses **social media** – this is the most powerful and cost effective tool for your marketing, why else would the Fortune 500 companies be there? LinkedIn, Facebook, Twitter, YouTube, Pinterest and Google+ to name the essentials, I believe, are the best for business owners. Understanding the etiquette of each of these is very important, as it changes with each platform. Branding yourself and your business is very important if you wish to monetise your time

and effort with social media. Be prepared to spend a certain amount of time a day on this medium, as it does work used correctly.

8. A good networker **brands** themselves – with all the changes in business today business owners have realised that they need to brand themselves with a consistent message. It is important to have 'good tools' in your tool box. Your business card and/or website are your shop window and the first thing many future customers see of you. So, make sure your website, blogs, e-newsletters, magazines, social media, business cards, etc. use the same story.

9. A good networker **goal sets** – without clear and concise goals no business can move forward into the future. So just as a business owner sets goals for his business, a good networker will also set goals for their networking outcomes. So, never go to a networking event without knowing what it is you want to achieve at that event.

10. A good networker asks questions for others – some small business people are hesitant to speak up and really say what they need. Some are even hesitant to speak up privately. For example, at a talk I was giving a business owner asked me a question about getting referrals. After the meeting I said, "Why did you ask that question? You already know how to do that, as you are a great networker." He said, "Yeah, I did, but a lot of other people didn't — and they

needed to hear the answer from you." Outstanding networkers have a feel for the issues and concerns of those around them and step up to ask questions others are hesitant to ask. So, support your fellow friends, clients and acquaintances.

11. A good networker knows that it is not who you know, but **who knows you** – becoming known both in your niche as well as outside it is imperative. Profiling people when they meet them is what they do all the time without even realising it. Never underestimate anyone you meet. You do not know who they are, who they know and who knows them. Make the world your friend and discover some incredible understated people.

12. A good networker **loves people** – this is the most important part of being a networker. If you don't like people, forget networking as it will show.

Networkers support, promote/sell others without even realising that they are doing it. It's their way of giving back for all that they receive. If you are an introverted person and find it difficult meeting new people or being in a room full of people, find a way and a process that you can use when you go to events. There are different strategies that work well for introverts.

"Don't find customers for your products, find products for your customers." - Seth Godin

AWESOME AUTHENTICITY

13
PROSPECTING VS NETWORKING

Always be the first to arrive at an event and one of the last to leave
- Jennie Gorman

AWESOME AUTHENTICITY

Frequently when attending networking events, I find that people are prospecting rather than networking, even though they have gone to a networking event. It appears that some people are unaware that there is a difference between the two.

Prospecting is when people go out to claim as many clients or contacts as they can so that they build their own business without any thought of what they have to offer the people they are meeting. Usually there is no getting to know or to understand the person they are meeting, let alone relationship building, to see if there is a synergy between them and their businesses.

When networking, it is important that you build your relationship firstly by listening and seeing where you can help or support them with what they are looking to achieve in their business. If you are really listening properly, it is not important to even talk about YOU and what YOU DO!

All relationships need to be win-win and if you help others to achieve their outcomes yours will be achieved in the long run too. People tend to feel that they need to support those who support them, so you will win in the end anyway.

Of course this goes back to understanding why you are business networking in the first place and what you are hoping to achieve from attending events.

Networking is something we need to be doing all the time … a seven day a week 'thing' that we automatically do with everyone we meet. It is not about pushing your product, service or company onto another, it is about developing a relationship so that the person gets to know you, who you are and what you stand for as a person.

People buy people they like and trust, so don't expect that they will automatically take what you are offering.

Good solid business relationships take time and effort to attain just as personal relationships do. It is a bit like dating … you don't expect on a first date to have a full blown relationship, so think of your networking in a similar way.

First, get to know the person, who they are, what they stand for while understanding what they do and how you can support them.

Not everyone you meet has a business whose services or products you need or want. By developing a relationship you will be able to learn about them and maybe support them with friends and clients that you know may want or need what they offer. This is true business networking.

It is all about supporting others first.

So, do you prospect or network when you go to events?

14
TEN TIPS FOR START-UP BUSINESSES

AWESOME AUTHENTICITY

Starting a new business is an exciting time for anyone who has a wish to do something that is their passion or has been a hobby. I find that many people who commence business for the first time have no actual structure and as a result make their start-up very difficult and with a propensity for failure.

Here are my 10 tips for those wishing to start a new business or someone who is revisiting their business structure.

1. Know why you want to create a business
2. Have a Vision for what you want your business to be in the future
3. Understand who your audience is and how you can reach them
4. Set up a solid platform/structure on how the business is to run
5. Systemise all aspects of the business
6. Create a basic Business Plan
7. Create a Financial Plan and have an Accountant
8. Create a detailed Marketing Plan including a Social Media/Advertising Plan
9. Create a 90 Day Action Plan every 90 days
10. Find a mentor and mastermind group to support you.

Now you can make these things happen by putting them into practice …

1 Know WHY you want to create a business

As mentioned previously, knowing your 'why' is one of the most important things you need to know before you start a business. If the passion is not there you will not be able to survive or sustain the rough times when business gets tough!

2 Have a Vision for what you want that business to be in the future

It is important that you have a clear and concise vision of where you see your business in 3 years and 5 years and beyond. If you do not have this, it is virtually impossible to be on track and focussed.

3 Understand who your audience is and how you can reach them

Knowing where your niche/audience is will show you where you can promote/pitch your business. You need to know where to go to meet your prospective clients. Having more than one niche is great once you have a business that is up and running, but for starters, stick with one in the beginning. It is much easier to target market.

4 Set up a solid platform/structure on how the business is to run

If you have no clear structure around your business it will be impossible for you to focus and prioritise what needs to be done to move forward. I suggest that you set very good documented procedures as this will give you the ability to leverage when you are ready.

5 Systemise all aspects of the business

This is critical if you are to have a smooth-running business. Technology has given us an easier and faster way to systemise our businesses so that others can come in and follow the process. You can then be away from your business and know that there is someone who can take the reins without too many challenges.

This is easier to do in the beginning than trying to do it after operating for years. If you are going to leverage in any way, it is imperative your systems are in place in all areas.

What would happen if for some reason you were unable to be at your business as a result of an accident or ill health? Could it sustain itself until you were able to be there again or could someone else take over for you?

This is a good question to consider and implement if your business could crumble without you. It could mean that your hard work would go to waste if someone could not take over the reins.

6 Create a basic Business Plan

A basic Business Plan will help guide you initially. Even though this is something that could easily go into the bottom draw, you need to have one to plan what you want your business to become in the future.

7 Create a Financial Plan and have an accountant

A financial plan for where you are now and for forecasting where you want to go is necessary. Find a good accountant who can guide you to set this in place. They will be worth it in the long run.

8 Create a detailed Marketing Plan including a Social Media/Advertising Plan

Once you know your marketplace you need to create a marketing plan for how you are going to get your message out to prospective clients. This covers your website, social media, advertising, business cards, flyers and the branding of your business.

9 Goal Set and create a 90 Day Action Plan every 90 days

Setting goals for the future is important and having a 90 Day Action Plan will keep you on track.

10 Find a mentor and MasterMind group for support

We all need to have someone to support us and keep us moving forward. A mentor/coach will help you but a business mastermind group will give you the on-going support 24/7 if necessary and give you your independent board of directors for future growth.

Of course there are more things you need to do but these are the basics to get your business moving. Start with these 10 and you will find a change in the way you see your business.

15
THE DIFFERENCE BETWEEN NETWORKING AND NETWEAVING

AWESOME AUTHENTICITY

Networking is a word well recognised by us all in business now, but **NetWeaving** is a relatively new concept in Australia. It is a step beyond the traditional business networking that people are doing now. The word NetWeaving was coined by Bob Littell, a consultant in the USA.

Networking, as we are all aware, is used traditionally to find new business and for creating or changing your career.

NetWeaving, in comparison, is a simple, more reciprocal approach that focuses on helping others meet the people they need to meet to solve their challenges, rather than their own.

This really is TRUE relationship building.

The difference between the two is their 'mind set'. Instead of looking for someone to help you with what you want, it is about you helping others get what they want!

Even though networking is known as an effective way of making new contacts for yourself, NetWeaving expands this as a long term tool that focuses on developing a reciprocal business relationship that will continue on for a very long time.

Do you want to improve your efficiency in the traditional approach? In the traditional networking approach, you go to a meeting or function with the idea of trying to gain strategic alliances that will help boost your business.

In other words, the mind-set is, "What's in it for me?" It's an effective means of making new contacts and developing business relations that can be very beneficial but there is a better, more lasting and trustworthy way.

NetWeaving differs slightly in its approach. To be a NetWeaver is to have the intent to learn all you can from as many people as possible about their businesses, their needs and challenges so that you can support them to find the contacts you have that can help them. The networker has the intent to learn what they can from someone to lead them to business for themselves, thus forgetting the other person!

The underlying theme of NetWeaving is the reciprocity. By supporting and doing good things for others, it can repay you many times over. I am sure that you will have noticed in your life that when you help others, good things seem to happen to you too.

The first big question you need to ask is: How can I help you? By starting your conversations when you meet people with a 'how can I help you?' question, the energy will totally change. You will find that there may even be a silence at first … People are not used to being asked that question.

Usually they are quick to tell you about themselves and usually don't stick around to hear about you.

How often does someone ask you a question like that? I have found it very rarely, and when I do, I know that I have found someone with a synergetic mind-set!

A more relaxed approach is here. Being a NetWeaver is much more relaxing and gives events or meetings a more human approach. There is nothing worse than watching people 'work the room' for opportunities to help themselves, knowing that they really aren't interested in what people are saying, unless it helps them achieve their goal. It appears sometimes that all they want is your business card so they can harass you later and move onto the next person as quickly as possible.

Showing your interest in people and genuinely wanting to learn about what they do and how you can help them, can change your experience around events. The person you are speaking with is looking for ways that your knowledge and experience can help them achieve what they want and need. Everyone is looking for the missing pieces of the puzzle, with problems that need to be solved. We have the opportunity to support others with their ideas that without someone else's help and support may never be created. **This is NetWeaving!**

None of us really is aware of how much we can help others until we start listening to what others need. With experience you will begin to learn to hear the words people say that 'ring a bell' for you so that you know how you can support them.

Everyone has a number of business contacts that they value, whom they know well enough to know their skills and strengths in different areas. By listening to what is being said in a conversation, you can ascertain very quickly who would be a good contact for the next step for that person. Ask yourself, 'could meeting or having contact with 'Bill' be beneficial?' Sometimes it might not be to get some work, but to help them achieve what they need to do for their next step.

You may ask yourself, 'has this person got the resources I could use for someone I know?' and/or 'would I consider adding them to my resource list'?

The two questions that always come to mind when I am referring someone is 'do I trust this person' and 'have they the integrity that I desire in my network?'

NetWeavers know the Golden Rule – they understand the laws of giving, sometimes called 'Givers Gain'. If you can give without expectation your world of networking will become a world of NetWeaving.

NetWeaving is based on helping others to achieve, knowing that 'what goes around, comes around'. They trust and have confidence in who they are and what they are doing. If you learn how to position yourself strategically for others by 'strategically people matching' you will become a perfect 'NetWeaver'.

'Paying it Forward' is another relatively new concept developed in the last few years that is starting to make its mark … it is all about NetWeaving. Have you read the book called *Pay It Forward* by Catherine Ryan Hyde? It is a book about a small boy who comes up with a simple idea which changes the world. The concept is, when someone does you a favour, rather than paying that person back, you 'pay it forward' and do a favour for someone else. It is a very simple concept and one that works.

NetWeaving is about enjoying helping others to achieve what they want. Have you ever noticed that when you do something for someone, you usually learn something?

Funny how that happens, isn't it?

As a NetWeaver do you :
- connect people with someone you know that they would benefit from meeting or knowing?
- provide information or resources to someone else who is from your own or another network?
- build your own "Trusted Resource Network" of people who are exceptional at what they do?

If you do the above, you have a great set of skills that will support you as a NetWeaver to achieve what you want and need.

So, instead of looking to be 'paid back', ask each person you have helped to 'pay it forward' and help someone else – either by making an introduction or offering resources. And of course, if you believe in the law of reciprocity, then you know that, "what goes around, DOES come around".

If NetWeaving sounds like something you would like to learn about – the skill set as well as strategies for building more NetWeaving into your daily routine by becoming more 'referable' yourself; I suggest you:
- get to know other like-minded people who genuinely share the NetWeaving philosophy;
- learn how to become a NetWeaver and eventually teach and train others.

The LENGTH of a person's life is not what counts ... it's the QUALITY of the content with which they fill it.

If you use this NetWeaving philosophy above in developing your relationships, you will find that it will add quality to you and your life.

AWESOME AUTHENTICITY

16
A REFERRAL NETWORK THAT GIVES YOU LEADS

AWESOME AUTHENTICITY

Building a business these days can be hard without the reputation and 'social proof' to support you. Many people in business feel that they can just create a business and the people will come. To make matters worse, many of these feel that they should be earning from the first week.

Why is it that people think they do not need to earn the right to get people's hard earned money?

The marketplace has been swamped in the last few years with people promising the world, at great financial cost, whom I believe sometimes are lacking integrity or authenticity. These people come often using internet marketing as the tool, promising the quick fix, and basically rape the people who do not do their due diligence and who get ripped off in the process. These fly-by-nighters then move onto another crowd and continue to do the same thing, hurting and damaging the trust and faith given them.

I believe that the marketplace is changing though. People are waking up and realising that their now limited hard earned dollars need to be spent well. By creating your own network of people, especially using business **mastermind groups** as your inner-circle, you can create and develop all the leads and skills you need to sustain your business growth.

Masterminding is POWERFUL! Develop a group of trusted advisors who will support you to not only grow your business but give you good sound business advice.

These groups are gold. **Mastermind groups** are about developing you and your business, with the support of others who have integrity and authenticity, who will keep you on track as well as accountable. If you find the right group, you can collaborate and gain sustainable joint ventures to reach your vision for your life and future.

17
HOW TO MAKE YOUR BUSINESS GROW IN THE FUTURE

Build your credibility using social media
— Jennie Gorman

AWESOME AUTHENTICITY

One of the things that many business owners find hard to achieve is working out their **niche market** and how to make their business grow in the direction they want. It is critical to identify **what the marketplace is looking for** and **what it is that you want to achieve**.

Your niche is the particular area/industry that you choose to focus on so that you can build your business fast. Once you have achieved the outcomes in one niche, you can then move onto another niche. Many businesses over a period of time have more than one niche. I have many but they have been built and nurtured consciously over many years.

Sometimes finding your right niche can be harder than it seems. We can become very blinded by our desire to go one way without realising it may not be the correct direction to go. We also are not always aware of what others are looking for and what they need to gain for their own business growth. Remember, they are looking for us as much as we are hoping to attract them.

For many of my clients and myself included, my format for **MasterMinding** (as I spell and write it for my business groups) has become a wonderful way to gain objective ideas from our peers. We are made accountable so we can create what we desire. By being in a solid group, which meets on a regular basis, you can move forward much faster than without this support. It is important to develop a special synergy and relationship with everyone in the group as this will move you and your business toward your particular outcomes and goals.

Mastering and honing the skills of **relationship building** gives you an opportunity to achieve your desired goals faster.

By finding your **niche marketplace** and developing relationships with other businesses you can then support them also to achieve their desired outcomes. By doing this, you will move closer to creating the opportunity for a joint venture or collaboration with like-minded businesses to help you grow too. If you spend time with people who come from a different perspective, with a different personality profile, you will find that your view will change and you will see things differently and gain ideas that you never thought of, let alone considered.

Today, **Social Media Marketing** (SMM) has become essential in the business world. The Fortune 500 companies would not be there if there weren't great benefits for them!! So, are you developing your skills and profile in this area too? This is the most powerful, easy, cost effective way to develop your business to heights you never imagined.

Having a **Mentor** or **Coach** can also be essential if you wish to move forward fast. This gives another dimension to looking at your business. Note that this is different to being in a mastermind group. **Mastermind groups** are not coaching sessions and/or networking or referral groups. Be aware that all successful business entrepreneurs around the world have their own mentor or coach to take them to their next level.

Successful business people use both **masterminding** and **mentoring** to move forward. They are aware that they need to develop both themselves and their business.

AWESOME AUTHENTICITY

18
MAKING A POSITIVE DIFFERENCE IS EASIER THAN YOU THINK

Without a clear vision you wont reach your potential

— Jennie Gorman

AWESOME AUTHENTICITY

It astounds me how difficult some people seem to think making a difference to another's life can be. Most people who are networking feel that they are creating **connections** for their business only, forgetting that what comes first is supporting people in achieving their needs, in all areas of their lives.

Networking gives you the opportunity to meet like-minded people who will not only be with you in business but maybe in your personal life too! As we grow and develop we find that many people we work with in our business become more than business acquaintances. As we build the trust and friendship, we can go to that next level of relationship.

How do you **make a difference** in other people's lives?

Are you listening to what others are saying and looking for?

Do you listen to what they are really asking when they speak with you?

No matter who we are or what we do, we all have needs that are not business related. So, do you really **listen** to what people are saying in regards to what they are looking for in their life to make it easier?

You may meet a good tradesperson, a book keeper or an accountant, find a great place to eat out for a special occasion, know where to get good stationery, something for their computer, or where to get a great Christmas present for their grandchildren.

Helping people get what they are wanting at that moment can create a relationship that can last for a long time. We all have a mixture of people in our network, so pass your good contacts around to those who deserve your network.

These people whom you connect with will become your NETWORK and your NETWORTH!! We are a reflection of the people in our life.

As you can see, people talk about all sorts of things that may not be anything to do with their business. This doesn't make the need any less than if it was business related!

So, you can **make a difference** to many people's lives by just **listening** to what they are looking to find and the contacts they need to make. Help them find that and you will build your network easily.

At this time we are fortunate for the internet and the creation of Social Media.

We are being given a wonderful opportunity to connect with more people, getting to know more about the 'friends' whom we personally know and are in our network. This gives us the chance to support even more than we could before.

To develop a good **relationship** for future success it is imperative that you are seen as someone who listens to the needs of your clients and contacts, supports them to find what they are looking for and become known as a person with good contacts.

Building **relationships** covers all areas, not just business.

So, think again about how you can help others in your **network** to achieve what they need outside of their businesses. Help them find the contacts they are looking to find. This is why learning more about your clients and contacts can support you to achieve what you are looking to find too!

Be the supporter that your network needs.

AWESOME AUTHENTICITY

19
BE MORE THAN GOOD, BE AWESOME ...

AWESOME AUTHENTICITY

Have you ever asked yourself how others see your business or how you feel about it yourself? Do your clients say you are good, or do they say you are **AWESOME**?

How do you want your clients and customers to remember you? What do you want them to say about you in general conversation?

These are important questions, so we get an idea of not only how we see ourselves but also how our clients and peers in the marketplace see us. If you have never asked these questions, get some testimonials or do a survey to get some good constructive feedback.

Ask your clients what areas or categories they see you as good, great or awesome in, and why do they say that? This is important for you to decide your correct niche, where you are going and if you are meeting and serving your correct marketplace. For me, as a small business owner, I do not judge a business necessarily by the amount of money that they create. I believe it is more on how your clients feel about you and if your services are giving them what is wanted and required.

Ask yourself who it is that you and your business want to serve?

It is also important to know what outcomes you want from your clients and your services/products? If you have a business that employs others, you need to make sure your bottom line is working in your favour as the dollar factor becomes more imperative, so you can pay not only your staff but yourself too!

It is wonderful to be described as good or great, or better still, awesome, but what does that mean? To achieve the title of being great or awesome doesn't only apply to large business, where there is staff and a strong management.

As a small business owner, this can apply to you too. We are seen on how good, great or awesome we are in our leadership skills.

How we connect and hold the vision for our business, no matter how large or small, will show through, too. We do not all want to have the large company or corporation. We can still play a big part in supporting our clients, by providing services and products that are right for them and their needs.

I believe that the only difference in a large or small business is the turnover and the number of people working both on it and in it. The skills necessary are still the same, just on a different level size wise.

I suggest that you learn who you are, what your leadership skills are and how they are received by others. If you hold your vision of what you set your business to be, looking at yourself and becoming accountable for the direction you have taken, you can only succeed, no matter your business size.

It is important that you see yourself and your business as two separate entities so that either can be removed and both stay intact.

Is this what you set out to do when you started your business? Or was it to create something that would close when you are no longer there to work it?

One of the things that affect a business, especially a small business, is when the person who heads it gets caught up in the glory of their business. Staying focussed on an end result without buying into the 'ego' will make your business strong and successful.

As a promoter of small business over many years, I have seen people who have had a great impact on others to such an extent that they got caught up in the belief that they were the only ones! We attract the people around us that we need so that we can help fulfil both our own and others hopes and desires in an area of their lives.

So, what and who do you want to be remembered by when you leave your business?

If you have a business that you want to grow and become a company that is known and respected, I suggest that you read *Good to Great* by Jim Collins. This book is also good for anyone in business to learn some good business principals too!

AWESOME AUTHENTICITY

20
CUSTOMER SERVICE THE BEST ADD-ON YOU CAN GIVE

AWESOME AUTHENTICITY

The maker or breaker of business is customer service. I experience bad customer service so often that it astounds me. How do people think they can stay in business if they do not look after the most important asset they have – their customers?

As Australians we are fairly apathetic and I can only assume that as many business owners are the same, they think that people are too lazy to do anything about changing where they do business for convenience sake. I often wonder if I am right in this assumption.

Social media has the power to put someone out of business very fast and many businesses have found this out to their own detriment.

At the beginning of each year we need to take the time to reflect by taking a good look at what we can do to create a better business in the future. There are two things that are lacking in many businesses today, that stand out to me above anything else, the lack of customer service and acknowledgement of their clients.

So, what can you do to add value to your business and have your clients talking about you?

I suggest that you ask yourself, "How can I create a better service for my customers and clients" without it costing an arm and a leg?

I believe with all the changes happening in business today we need to become more aware and pro-active if we wish to succeed. So I suggest that you start to use your imagination by becoming creative so that you can stand out from others around you.

Are you acknowledging the people who are your customers already?

Can you do more for them?

Are you aware of how to make their experience with you a better one than they get with others?

What do you do that is different so they will talk about you and your business?

Are you acknowledging their importance to you and your business verbally or with tokens or gifts?

Word of mouth marketing (networking/relationship building) is the most powerful way to make your business grow, especially if your dollars are limited.

When I shopped prior to last Christmas for stocking fillers for my grandchildren, I became aware of the lack of customer service in many of the larger shops.

Even though I chose a beautiful new store, with large aisles and plenty of stock, I was highly critical of their lack of staff and service to the customers they were wishing to attract. Even though their shelves were bulging, there was no one around to help support their customers. I left the store with only one article when I was looking to fill a trolley!

I was overwhelmed when I ended up at another well-known low cost store in the same complex, where I found staff in many aisles, ready to help, with an understanding of not only their stock but where to find it. I saw them helping their customers find whatever they were looking to buy, proving why their bottom line is now very healthy! They obviously have good training for their staff in understanding their customer's needs and excellent staff incentive schemes!

Of course when shopping at Christmas time, children let you know what they want a long way prior to the event, but as the adult, you wonder, what am I looking for and where do I find it? The first store missed out on my hundreds of dollars and the second store gained them and I was the grateful shopper.

If you are like me, and dislike shopping, customer service is always gratefully appreciated and recognised.

Being a business 'people networker' I chatted to people as I walked around myself and supported them where I could too, knowing how frustrating this time of the year can be. The one thing that I did do was tell others of my experience with other stores where there was a lack in certain areas! Good 'word of mouth marketing' for the customer, not so good for one particular store!

So, where is your point of difference going to be?

AWESOME AUTHENTICITY

21
RELATIONSHIP MARKETING CAN TAKE YOU TO THE NEXT LEVEL

AWESOME AUTHENTICITY

Running a small business, especially if it is from home or an office with little or no staff, can be a very lonely place. For many, it is hard to understand the importance of working 'on' your business against working 'in' your business.

To develop a strong and flourishing enterprise, an owner needs to be able to attract people and other businesses to use their products or services. I find that most small businesses are what I call 'luxury businesses', which in the competitive marketplace of today, are even harder to market. A luxury business from my point of view is one that others can live without or can wait to use, as they are not necessary for survival.

My experience has shown me that to take your product and services to the marketplace successfully, you need support to make that happen. Being involved in a mastermind group or similar can move you and your business toward your goal faster than you imagined.

Masterminding can help you build strong relationships that can support you to accomplish what you are wanting from your business. It will focus you, keep you accountable and move you forward by giving you the skills and contacts necessary to develop you and your business, if you find the right group. **This is known as 'working-on' your business!**

This small group of other entrepreneurs will become your building block to grow your business. This can be a far more economical way to spread the word without spending the big dollars on advertising, etc.

Learning how to use social media as a marketing tool has given us all the opportunity to really create business relationships in an easier format than ever before. For me personally, over 90% of my business comes via social media and meet-up groups. Masterminding can help you use this more successfully in your business development.

So, if you want to stand out in the marketplace, find yourself a good mastermind group, understand your niche market and build your contacts from there. Don't spread your wings too far initially and focus in on where your particular clients are going to be. If you become known and trusted for what you do, you will in time develop what you want.

Remember, this is not a hit and miss way of creating your clients. This is to support you to develop a very strong base of people, who, if your products and services are of good value, will recommend you to others along the way.

It is important when building your business relationships to understand that you are not there to 'push yourself, your products and services down someone else's throat'. It is necessary to build the trust level so that you have people talking about you and what you do.

I have found that masterminding is the best way to build strong relationships with a small group of other business people. These business entrepreneurs will really get to know you, know your products and services, and support you to achieve what you want to achieve.

As Napoleon Hill, Pioneer of Personal Achievement Philosophy said:

"The moment you commit and quit holding back, all sorts of unforeseen incidents, meetings and material assistance, will rise up to help you. The simple act of commitment is a powerful magnet for help."

AWESOME AUTHENTICITY

22
WHY RESILIENCE IS IMPORTANT IN RELATIONSHIP BUILDING

AWESOME AUTHENTICITY

This may seem a very strange comment, and from my understanding of relationship building, being resilient is having the quality of being able to be bent and stretched in all directions whilst being able to bounce back to your original form, when the pressure is off.

We need to be able to do this to achieve what we want to achieve, especially when developing new relationships, as we are all different. Being flexible is so important when we are in business today. Being able to see another's point of view and recognising that the way they think is just as important to them, as your point of view is to you.

So, how resilient are you? Being resilient comes in many forms and learning how to bounce back is very important. Dealing with hardship and being able to hold your head high and staying honest to yourself is number one.

As business owners we need to learn to be tough on the inside, to have 'stickability' and not fold when things get hard. We will meet all types of people so we need to be able to communicate from where they are to develop a successful relationship for the future, if we want to do so.

Learning to cope when life throws us a curveball is not always easy. Sometimes it takes experience and courage to be able to stand tall and shrug off what sometimes can hurt us deeply.

Learning to stand up for oneself, in business can be difficult. Being resilient shows people around us how we deal with adversity and will give a very big picture of us as an individual to those who are wondering how we cope with difficult times. In business partnerships this is a very important factor when choosing someone to work with closely.

I am sure you are aware, like most of us these days in business, that there will be many ups and downs as a normal part of living. As business owners we suffer from more stresses and traumas in life than ever before. Our world is moving so fast today, and we have to be able to keep up and learn how to manage each crisis as they will come in many forms.

We see this in the extraordinary number of people struggling with depression, people who work too long hours and those who have not learned how to be resilient. For me, I was fortunate to learn this skill very early in life and will be forever grateful to my parents as it has stood me in good stead over many years.

We need to understand that we are all different and our challenges in life are unique to us as individuals, as our experiences would not have been the same and our learnings from childhood were different too. We find that everyone has different resources for coping and how long it takes anyone to bounce back from things that are stressful to them will be a result of their past experiences.

Do not judge others on how you as an individual react to things. Be aware and acknowledge that others will react differently through their tough times and do your best to support them when and if you can. Learning how you yourself cope with the stresses and strains of life can support you to be even more resilient in the future.

Research has shown that many factors and circumstances in life promote how resilient we are. It may be a supportive and stable family, we might have a positive and optimistic view about life and/or a good sense of worth. The groups that we belong to also make a difference, with good friendships and our sense of belonging being a large factor. Our positive relationships with people we care about is usually evident in the way we deal with crises too.

Resilient people see opportunities in all things, accept change as a part of living, they keep things in perspective by being realistic, they maintain positive relationships, they find strategies to support themselves when things are tough, and they take action to achieve what they want. Resilient people are happy to talk and get help when they are struggling with life, and importantly, they develop an attitude of tolerance, acceptance and flexibility.

There are of course many more behaviours and factors that are common in how we cope with life. Do you understand and see where your resilience comes from?

If you are struggling and wondering how you can develop a more resilient life I would suggest that you develop a better self-awareness by understanding how you cope emotionally with 'you' when you have a crises, by being aware of how you react to it. More than likely it is a learned behaviour from your younger years that does not serve you now that you are an adult.

AWESOME AUTHENTICITY

It is important that you understand your needs, joys and frustrations, your goals, values and beliefs whilst understanding your individual limits. If you can view your life from a bigger picture, away from your challenges, this will help you. By understanding how you 'self-control' and when you do not, is a major factor in watching your behaviour. If you know your strengths and responses to situations that affect you, you will understand how you can change any current behaviour that is not serving you.

Your style of coping relates usually to your early learning history. What your 'habit' was as a child, (as discussed in the Enneagram – a personality profiling system) that supported you to gain what you wanted from life, is not self-serving as an adult. In fact, it can be very destructive to you and your relationships. For information on the Enneagram I suggest that you go to: http://enneagram.com.au

May your future bring you an ability to be able to move through your challenges in life easier by understanding what makes you who you are and what serves you better.

23
NETWORKING VS. MASTERMINDING

Business networking is a wonderful way to build your profile and add to your business leads and contact list. For most people business networking is a 'hit and miss' experience because they do not understand many of the necessary skills that are needed to help them grow their business.

My model of masterminding on the other hand is structured. This model creates accountability, gives participants the ability to grow their business faster and more accurately than they will ever get through networking. You will become more effective and efficient, be more productive and motivated than ever before.

From my experience of running mastermind groups I have found that they outrank **networking** to such an extent that there is no comparison. They are two totally different experiences.

There are many external factors that affect the well-being of a small business. By networking you need to understand what you want so you can determine the outcome you wish to have from the experience. Many of these networking events are beyond our control and can be adverse or positive, dependent on how a business owner responds.

Using masterminding instead of networking can generate the outcome for the business in a more far-reaching positive and unique way. The support to move to the next level is inevitable. Controlling your responses is much easier than controlling events. Individual accountability in business has a significant role in its rise and fall.

Over the last 10+ years technological growth has invaded both our personal and professional lives. We have choices with these advancements in space, technology, internet, television, smart phones and more. So, all small business owners need to become as aware and informed as possible.

Social media gives everyone the opportunity to build contacts far easier than ever before. It is important to understand what the best platforms for you to use are so you can achieve your wanted outcomes.

For small business to survive in the market today, it is necessary that they need to bank on their own skills and abilities by becoming aware of their own economic viability.

Do not expect opportunities to just happen if you are not able to provide value to others. This is the first basic lesson that you must consider when it comes to accountability in business. Being part of a mastermind group will move you and your accountability forward very fast, as long as the structure in the group is there to support all participants.

Be aware that your business will depend on your actions – whether negative or positive. If you are a solo entrepreneur or small business owner, you will find being supported by others, who can give ideas, advice and support by creating accountability, will not only help you to develop yourself personally but also your business.

It is necessary that you keep networking strategically to meet new people to continue to create a wider network. By bringing a mastermind group into your strategy you can only have a very positive win-win which I believe will outdo any type of basic networking.

By being part of a **business mastermind group** and having the benefits of other people who will keep you accountable and moving forward is not only beneficial but a gift. If the group is synergised well, you have your independent board of directors, who will be with you and your business for the long term. The personal friendships that come via masterminding is something that is totally unforeseen.

AWESOME AUTHENTICITY

24
THE ULTIMATE TOOL FOR BUSINESS SUCCESS

Have you ever wondered, if you are a small business person, how you can build your business to its fullest potential successfully on your own? I am telling you, you can't. Ask Richard Branson or any other highly successful business person how they have done it and who they have needed to take them to the heights that they have achieved.

For any business to achieve all it is capable of, it needs many skills. This means it will need expertise in areas of direction, administration, sales and marketing, accounting, etc. No one person can achieve all these on their own. We all have our own exceptional skills and innate gifts, be they creative and/or logical in form. It is important to understand what and where your strengths are and the challenges in your business.

Do you know who you need to help you to develop yourself, as well as your business to take it to the next level? As mentioned previously, I know that **masterminding** for a small business person is the best and most economical way to go about achieving the needs for a business's future. Participants will be given the opportunity to have their own 'Board of Directors' (meaning the other participants in the group) who can and will support, challenge and make you accountable, so that can move your business forward.

For the solo entrepreneur, business has many ups and downs as well as being sometimes a very lonely place. If you happen to not be in a personal relationship or have a good support group around you, it can become even more difficult and challenging when it comes to decision making, financial areas, ill health, etc.

As a result of being in a **mastermind group** some of the benefits you will achieve will be an instant and valuable support network, giving you a sense of shared endeavour in understanding you are not alone. It is important to learn how to work 'on' your business, and not only 'in' it, as happens with most small business owners who are not in a position to employ staff.

Finding a masterminding group, a coach or mentor will give you real growth in your business and personal life, giving you the opportunity to design and create YOUR business the way you want it.

Masterminding does also give wonderful opportunities for collaboration and joint ventures. Having a good coach or mentor also can support you to find the people you need to get the results you want, if they are well connected.

To gain the above you need to not only to be highly motivated to achieve your goals to go to the next level, but to learn to ask for what you need and be prepared to give help and support as required.

If you decide on being part of a **business mastermind group** it needs to be a win-win relationship, fun for all participants with a total commitment to the group.

The opportunity to develop and create your goals for your future are in your hands as a result of the support you will receive by going to this next level.

25
WHY IS MASTERMINDING SO POWERFUL?

AWESOME AUTHENTICITY

You have heard many times previously that **business networking** is a wonderful way to build your profile and add to your business leads and contact list. For most people in business, networking is an experience that doesn't work well. This is because of a lack of understanding of networking skills needed to help grow any business.

Learning the skills you need to acquire, as an individual to grow your business, can be done by anyone if you know where to get the information.

MasterMinding on the other hand, if it is structured and creates accountability, will give a participant the ability to grow their business far faster and more accurately than they will ever get through networking. You become more effective and efficient, more productive and much more motivated than ever before.

From my experience of facilitating my Business MasterMind Groups over some years now, I have found that they out rank networking to such an extent that there is no comparison.

There are many external factors that affect the well-being of a small business which networking alone can't support.

The response to the way those using networking to relationship build will determine the outcome. It is necessary to participate fully to achieve what you want.

Using masterminding to strengthen and build your relationships for future success can only generate the outcome for the business in a positive and unique way as the relationship building is deeper and stronger.

The support in these mastermind groups to move to the next level is inevitable. Controlling your responses is much easier than controlling events. Individual accountability in business has a significant role in its rise and fall.

We are all aware of how technology has taken over our lives in all areas be it personal or business. We do not have a choice NOT to embrace it as we will be left behind.

We moved from the agricultural age in the very early 1900s to the industrial revolution of manufacturing. We are now in the early stage of the technological world of computers, so I suggest that you embrace it and make it work for you. There is no time now for anyone's 'head in the sand' or 'I do not want to know' thoughts. It is a make or break time for businesses to become technological in all areas.

The world is now global ... business is now global. It is time to think out of the box and expand. Hiring virtual staff both nationally and internationally is a thing that is becoming the norm. Understand it and make it work for you and your business. Most small business people can't afford not to do this now as our workloads increase dramatically. From a cost effective perspective, international outsourcing is a must.

For small business to survive in the market today it is necessary that they need to bank on their own skills and abilities by becoming aware of their own economic viability. Do not expect opportunities to just happen, if you are not able to provide value to others. This is the first basic lesson that you must consider when it comes to accept accountability in business.

Masterminding will move you and your accountability forward very fast, as long as the structure in the group is there to support all participants. It will also make your productivity expand which means you have a choice of going it alone or hiring staff. Initially, virtual staff can help. A business owner needs to learn how to use them correctly and efficiently to find the key to being successful in this area. This is a subject all on its own.

Be aware that your business will depend on your actions – whether negative or positive. If you are a solo entrepreneur or small business owner, you will find being supported by others who can give ideas, advice and support by creating accountability, will not only make you develop yourself but also your business.

Remember, **business networking** needs to be strategic and by bringing a mastermind group into your strategy you can build on your own community and network. By being part of a **business mastermind** group you will have the benefit of other people who will keep you accountable and on track. They will support you in those times when you doubt yourself or become aware of your lack of knowledge and expertise. They have the ability to see your business from another perspective as we are all far too close to our businesses to open our peripheral vision when we sometimes need to.

The power of a mastermind group, which supports you to become real, accountable and open, by developing a trust that can't be measured, will be the thing that will support you to realise your dreams and vision for your business.

26
WANT TO MOVE YOUR BUSINESS FORWARD?

AWESOME AUTHENTICITY

Every business owner, I am sure, would want to succeed in their business endeavours. If they have a dream and a vision for their business, they will have a hunger for its growth. There must be a passion for their business so that their success is forthcoming.

We all want to develop and continually grow in order to catch up with the rapidly changing business world. It is inevitable that we encounter problems and trials that will test the strength of not only our business but us as people too. In order to be prepared to face those upcoming problems, it is recommended that you have a support group. These are the people who will walk with you through your challenges and share your successes in an honest and caring way. This is where **mastermind groups** become valuable if you are to succeed as a small business person.

I know from experience that a mastermind group can do that for you by giving you the support necessary for your business future. It is all about how the group is put together and the conditions and etiquette that are part of the process.

You have now been reading about **mastermind groups** quite a bit, and now you may ask, what really is a **MasterMind Group**?

My process is different from others so I can only talk about how I do it. There are many people who run groups and they all serve a similar purpose. I believe to be effective there needs to be certain protocols around the process. For me, I want to bring a group of selected business owners together who I know will have a certain synergy. These are people who want to grow their business to the next level fast.

They come together to:
- talk and discuss who and where they are;
- understand their business vision and mission;
- create their own structured goal plan for growth;
- better understand their business needs;
- get support with their challenges;
- gain and increase the skills they need;
- broaden their skill set;
- develop a better business mind-set;
- discover what they do best in their business;
- and, move their business to the next level.

Of course there is much more to the groups than this. By these discussions above they find out how they can best help and serve each other to have the outcomes each member is there to achieve. The sessions are very structured so that everyone's needs are met.

The unique thing about a mastermind group is that every member wants nothing but to help other participants grow, as well as their own business. The group objective is to guarantee that every participant will succeed in business through the support and accountability factor within the group. I have processes in place that keep this happening.

Commitment is one of the most valued qualities of a mastermind group. Every member should be committed to join and attend all meetings and activities. In this way, no one will miss out on the progress and development of every member in the group. To make sure that each group would function well, a selection and screening process is made prior to joining the group. In this way, each member of the group has more things in common and establishing connection will be easier.

My groups are closed groups, who meet fortnightly for six months. In every meeting we discuss and follow through with each other our progress and developments over the previous fortnight.

They discuss and follow through the topics talked about in the previous meeting and what outcomes as a result have happened in the progression. The group will discuss their strengths, weaknesses, opportunities and business threats. In this way, they brainstorm any challenges and have organised activities for further learning, that creates a win-win situation for every member.

Having a group of people who are committed to support you will surely push you forward. Being a part of a group is not only a good strategy for your business, but it is also a good way to have good emotional support. You can discuss, share and compare experiences about your life and your business as you wish. The best thing about masterminding is that others in the group know exactly what you mean and feel, as they are all in the same situation of growing and learning.

AWESOME AUTHENTICITY

27
BENEFITS OF MASTERMINDING

Authenticity is allowing the masks to come down
— Jennie Gorman

AWESOME AUTHENTICITY

Masterminding groups are nowadays quite common and held around the world using various names.

I personally like to stick to the original concept created by **Napoleon Hill** in his book ***Think and Grow Rich*** by keeping to the basic values he talks about.

"No two minds ever come together without thereby creating a third, invisible intangible force, which may be likened to a third mind."

The popularity of masterminding has been growing as many people these days are in business and want to find their own success recognising that they need some support. By sharing inputs and ideas with other individuals, creating visions and goals, and encouraging a positive mindset, a broader outlook can be perceived and attained.

Being involved in a mastermind group is also a great way to offer and receive support and input from another's perspective as they work to find a specific purpose and outcome. It helps individuals connect with others who share the same desires, interests and visions. They offer their ideas to others while receiving solutions and perspectives from the most unexpected individuals at the same time.

As part of his research work, **Napoleon Hill** wrote in his book ***Think and Grow Rich,*** masterminding brings together the *"coordination of knowledge and effort, in a spirit of harmony, between two or more people, for the attainment of a definite purpose."*

To make it simpler, a mastermind group is a union of two or more individuals dedicating themselves to fulfill a specific goal. I have found that six people in a group creates a greater balance of skill-sets if these people have the correct synergy.

As mentioned, a group can be as small as two to four individuals or as big as the facilitator can manage. I personally feel that the person running a group (the facilitator) cannot be part of the group for all present to get the benefits required from the group.

Mastermind groups also have two basic aims:
- focussing on an individual's success and vision
- focussing on helping everyone in the group.

Business MasterMind groups have many benefits and advantages also. They help you to succeed because you have a group of people available to help you. You also get the benefit of being able to hear and learn from the different feedback, input and opinions, whilst you share your own. This is somewhat a 'give and take' relationship in the process.

A mastermind group is also about growth and development. It helps you enhance your skills. It requires you to expand out of your comfort zone so that you will get the outcome that you truly want and need. It allows you to have a bigger and greater vision which gives you the motivation to achieve your goals. It helps you gain more confidence and helps borrow on the experience and skills of others. It also adds a supportive network.

There are still many **benefits of masterminding** and you'll experience it once you join a **mastermind group**, sharing with others your vision.

So, for you to have these benefits and experience though the power of masterminding I suggest that you join a group as soon as possible and see the difference. I suggest that you search the internet to find one that will give you the opportunity to achieve your goals.

The wisdom found within a group is astounding and has the ability to change not only your business but your life as well.

AWESOME AUTHENTICITY

28
ACCOUNTABILITY IN BUSINESS

AWESOME AUTHENTICITY

Accountability is not only necessary in life but in business and is what sets you apart from others. It is very important for you to have accountability in your business if you are to move forward in the future. I have found that masterminding with a group of business people is the greatest support you can have in business. It will open your mind and extend your thinking far above what you ever conceived on your own.

There are many external factors that affect the wellbeing of your business and your response to those events will determine the outcomes. Many of these events are beyond our control and can be adverse or positive.

What you can do is control your response to these events and generate the outcome for your business in a positive and unique way. Controlling your responses is much easier than controlling events. Individual accountability in business has a significant role in its rise and fall.

In these modern times there are many technological changes that have invaded our personal and professional lives. We are lucky as we now have so many choices with the advancements in space, technology, internet, television and more.

The world has become a smaller place thanks to the above technological developments. With them you are more aware and informed. There is also a negative aspect and many people believe that they are entitled to receive many benefits without the need to work for them. These benefits are relative and they differ from one person to another. It is this sense of entitlement that often proves a major hindrance in the development and progress of a business.

If this resonates, the first thing that you need to do is get rid of the sense of entitlement. In order for you to survive in the market you need to bank on your own skills and abilities. You must be aware of your economic viability. You should not expect opportunities to come your way if you are not able to provide value to others. This is the first basic lesson that you must consider when it comes to being accountable in business.

The buck stops with you! Your business is your business. Do not expect others to see it as you do. It is important though to have the people around and working with you understanding your vision and where you want your business to develop in the future. If your staff, clients and contacts understand your vision, and what you want to achieve, the more likely you are to achieve it.

When you are running a business you should never hold people accountable for the final specific outcomes. They have their part to play in your business or project and you need to leave them to do what they do, as long as you make sure they are on the right track for the next part to continue.

In order to make your business successful you must never hold other people accountable for **all the outcomes**, only for their part in it. They are already being accountable for the duties assigned to them. It is not right to blame them for the outcome of your business.

The consequences of your business will depend on your actions – negative or positive.

It is true that others you are working with in your business may act for you or cover your accountability; however, sooner or later these are the ones that will catch up with you and overtake you and your business.

Controlling those working for you will not help and the best thing that you could do is work in partnership with them. Giving them support in the outcomes they seek will help you get the support you need for your business to develop and expand. You are then giving value to one another and in the process the business benefits.

The risks are less and the rewards are more!

By being part of a **mastermind group** you have the benefits of a small group of people who will keep you accountable and moving forward. Understanding that this type of group is there to help you open your mind and peripheral vision so that you can see more clearly from others perspectives what you are hoping to achieve.

AWESOME AUTHENTICITY

29
GET YOUR OWN BOARD OF DIRECTORS

Mastermind groups give you your board of directors

— Jennie Gorman

This is one of the most significant parts of being with a group of external people who support you in your business growth. You may be asking yourself, what does getting my own 'board of directors' mean and if you are not aware of the mastermind concept, it may not mean anything to you.

Business masterminding is all about being with a group of like-minded people who want to move both you and their own business forward to a higher level than they are at now. To do this we need to have a sounding board … and this can be made up of people who have complementary skills and experiences that can support growth. Being in a mastermind group that has good resources and contacts, accountability, confidentiality and a variety of skill sets will move a business very fast.

The advantage of a mastermind group is the support received in return for the support given. This group of people will become trusted advisors, who you will be able to share your business with on an intimate level. They will keep you accountable and hold you to account so you can achieve where you want to go.

These trusted advisors will have a strong sense of what your business is all about, which can only develop though the integrity that will be created within the group synergy.

The opportunity to connect with potential clients and have some strong referral partnerships are benefits that spin off this process.

Even though mastermind groups are not coaching or mentoring groups, they act in a similar way as the group of people around you will keep you on track. So, instead of having one person, you have a group, which amplifies the success rate even higher, giving you a variety of perspectives to see what you want and where you are going.

Masterminding is the most cost effective, fast way to build your business. Paying for this privilege of being in a group makes it work, as it makes you accountable to this process.

30
MILLION DOLLAR LASTING RELATIONSHIPS

AWESOME AUTHENTICITY

What are your relationships worth to you? Until we develop one that has all the ingredients that support us to achieve what we wish to achieve, we do not recognise the value of them and where they can take us in the future.

To build a strong relationship that is going to establish a good outcome in the future, we need to develop a strong level of **TRUST**. This is not something that just happens. It takes time and patience to develop the rapport that is necessary for future success for both parties.

For a relationship to have the opportunity to develop into something that will bring value to all parties, each person needs to understand the value of trust within themselves.

So, I ask you … **where is your level of self-trust?** Unless you have that within yourself, you cannot find it in another. To have trust we need to be able to rely on the other party to do what they say they will do or bring to the situation.

Trust is the foundation for all effective communication in relationships. As we discover trust in someone we hope to do business with, we come from both an emotional and logical mind, which exposes both parties to being vulnerable. If we do not trust our self, we can't trust someone else.

So, how do people see you when they first meet you? Do you give out a feeling of being someone who the other person straight away wants to befriend and tell you their secrets? Or does it take some time for people to feel that connection?

Trust is all about knowing yourself and how authentic you come across to people meeting you for the first time. Do you give the feeling to others that you are someone who can be relied upon and can keep your word? Do you have faith and belief in others? Can you be relied upon to do the right thing? Do you have stickability to weather the tough times that come with all relationships?

Be aware that people will view you by the company you keep and what is perceived as your established reliability. We are a reflection of the people we have around us and this is what will give us our credibility or lack of it. Having positive people who want to grow and create something greater than they have at the present moment, are the people to be around, for you and your future growth. We are judged by society, rightly or wrongly, by the people we are connected to and where we share our time and energy. So, be aware of how you are seen in the marketplace.

Once a relationship has developed the 'trust level' that is necessary for moving forward, it is then that good collaboration, joint ventures, partnerships and/or new businesses start. If the synergy within the relationship is solid, reliable, honest and built on trust, the ability to go anywhere with this encounter is limitless. As long as the skillsets are complimentary, there is no reason for future success to not happen.

I believe 'The Key to Business Success' is attracting into our business only those we resonate with … so I ask you, **what and who are you resonating with?**

To really know someone, is to watch their behaviour with people they employ or how they treat people when they are in a restaurant or out for coffee. Do they treat others with respect and as equals, or do they regard themselves as better than people whom they feel are below or above them? It takes only a few moments to ascertain where someone sits when it comes to this.

So, become aware so that you can create the million dollar relationships you desire for your future.

AWESOME AUTHENTICITY

31
HOW TO SET YOUR GOALS AND MAKE THEM A REALITY

Goal setting gives you the opportunity to achieve your dreams

- Jennie Gorman

Setting a goal and then making it a reality are two different things. It is easy to set the goals, as most people who have ever made a new year's resolutions will know. Making them happen is another thing.

Goal setting is all about firstly setting goals that are **specific, attainable, realistic, achievable, measureable, contain emotion and give rewards**. I find that if you have a group supporting you, then you are more than likely to achieve your goals, as the group will keep you motivated and supported, so that you can achieve what you set out to do. **Accountability is one of the main aims of a good group.**

A **mastermind group** will help you be accountable for your goal setting and this is where the correct group for you will be life and business changing. Being able to share your goals and dreams with others, will keep you on track to achievement. No one likes to appear a failure, so a group will encourage and support you to achieving if you let them.

Knowing your life and business Vision and Mission will help you to vocalise it to your mastermind group. This is one of the first important steps to take. Document this so you can keep yourself on track.

I suggest an Action Plan that is broken up into 3-month cycles. All the steps that any goal will have need to be broken into bite sized chunks. It can be quite overwhelming to visualise a goal in its entirety, but broken down into easy steps helps make it a reality and more easily accomplishable.

Then you need to set the goals that you want to achieve to reach both the vision, with the mission steps clearly planned out. Your vision is the picture you see in your head/mind that you want to create in your world. The mission is the work you need to do to create that vision. A completion date when you will achieve each milestone is important too.

The goals you need to achieve must be set in their individual areas … next 3 months, 6 months, 12 months, 3 years and maybe 5 years. As the world is changing so fast, 10-year goals are a long way out, but it is good to see the future and have them in place too so you can move towards your vision easily.

Remember, it is important that you have a start and finish date for each part of your goal. This way you become obliged to achieve what you set out to do.

Brainstorming and discussion around each goal will be effective in helping you gain the information, resources, suppliers and maybe the money you need. It is easier and quicker to do this with a group than wasting time trying things out that may, in the long term, take you much longer to achieve. Use your mastermind group to short circuit and create what you want quicker. Do not try to reinvent the wheel … most things have been done in the past so find out how you can plug into others expertise to realise what you want.

It is important at each mastermind group session that you review your action plan so that you all keep on track.

Your achievements are important to your group and if each participant is achieving, it means that your group is flowing and a success.

AWESOME AUTHENTICITY

32
DON'T ASK YOURSELF WHAT THE WORLD NEEDS

AWESOME AUTHENTICITY

"Don't ask what the world needs, ask yourself what makes you come alive" is a saying that I love.

I talk a lot about 'doing what makes your heart sing' when I am presenting talks and workshops. So, I am asking you now ... Are you doing what makes YOUR heart sing?

Our passion is what shows when we talk and is in our actions for everyone you come in contact to see. Is your passion showing?

For me, I love helping people build good solid relationships and showing them how to do word-of-mouth marketing successfully. I feel great satisfaction when I know that I have connected two people, who may not have ever meet, who find the synergy that will help them move forward in either their personal life or the business world.

We are so blessed these days that we have the internet and that social media marketing has become such a way of life for many of us. Of course, we need to learn the balance of not getting too caught up in SMM (social media marketing) that we find time runs out for other important things. I suggest to people that they find a time of the day that they can do the SMM without doing it ad hoc and wasting a lot of time.

There are people in the marketplace who teach how to do this, so find out who they are and connect with them in this area if you need the support. Becoming aware of the platforms that work best for you and your business is imperative too.

I value the relationships that I have made via social media. Many of these relationships have become and developed into significant personal and business relationships via coffee or dinner meetings, networking events, workshops and mastermind groups. Many have become close and personal and share my world away from business. These relationships have been win-win and supported us both to achieve what we are wishing to achieve and have taken my life to another dimension.

I often ask people if they need help to move forward and reach the right people. If you want support with your networking, I suggest that you make a point of getting to know a networker. They will always support your progress if it is in their power to do so.

Enjoy what you are doing with your relationship building and, most importantly, make your heart sing, too!

33
THE POWER OF VISION

AWESOME AUTHENTICITY

The most incredible power we have as a human being is our **power of vision**. Most people go through life without realising that if there is something that they really want to do or have, all they have to do is imagine it and it will be created. The intentions they put on this is often the opposite of what they really want to manifest.

So, I wonder what your vision is. Do you have one? Do you believe it is achievable?

Your vision must be clear and concise for it to be manifested exactly as you see it in your thoughts.

To create your own vision for your life can be empowering and give you the sense of doing something outstanding using your own innate God given gifts. If the vision is to make a difference in the world, no matter what it is, your passion will fuel it into something even bigger and brighter.

We attract to our lives what we think about and what we put out through our thoughts, words and deeds. So, are you using the law of attraction to have what is yours?

When your vision is clear, precise and exact it becomes a seed that will grow as it is watered.

How you water it with your thoughts and actions is what will create it to flourish. It will become something that will transform many that come into contact with it, in their journey of life, no matter how positive or negative that thought is.

The world of quantum physics and neuroscience have come together to explain how this happens.

In quantum physics one learns to understand how our small world operates, even though we cannot see it with our own eyes. Our world is broken into two parts ... one we can see and the other we can't.

Science has proven that these two are interconnected at all levels even if we can't see them, or totally understand the connection.

Isaac Newton's physics shows us how to navigate our physical world while quantum physics helps us to understand the non-physical world of total connectedness.

Quantum research has taught us to understand that whatever we focus on and become emotional about, will be manifested. So, by focusing on your vision, the easier and faster it will become real, in your physical reality, acting like a magnet to create what you have created in your mind, whether good or bad.

As everything is vibration, know that a positive vibration creates the goodness around you and a negative vibration will manifest things you do not want to have in your life. We become whatever or whomever we surround ourselves with, as our environment makes us who we are. You will attract whatever vibration level you are playing on. By focusing our brain on what we really want, we can attract what we want by automatically increasing the amps of our cellular vibration.

The universe creates by natural law, precisely and in perfect order, what we put out into the world. The more we can KNOW what we want, the easier it is to manifest, no matter how big the gap is between where we are now and where we want to go. It will always come together, if we focus on the vision, as natural law will fill the gap automatically.

So, it is important that **YOUR intentions are pure**, as you can only create what you imagine. The vision you have in your mind will become real when you power it up as best you can so that the universe can manifest what you want in all areas of your life.

Choose wisely what you want, because it will become YOUR reality.

AWESOME AUTHENTICITY

34
AWESOME ABUNDANCE

AWESOME AUTHENTICITY

My world is like a box of chocolates … so full of abundance in so many forms.

How abundant is your life? What are you grateful for that not only touches your life, but others and their lives too? Are you showing the world who you really are?

I live in gratitude. My values and the way I have lived my life have been based on the blessings given me by the teachings that have come down from my family line. I come from four proud family lines from both my parents, who were men and women of great honour and integrity. I feel very blessed to have had such important role models.

Abundance comes in so many ways … it flows throughout our lives in all moments in a spiritual, creative self-caring way. Our relationship with self and others, as well as from others perspectives, are measured by our abundance eg financial, health, life's basics, etc. It radiates from us through our life in how we express our joy, beauty, peace and love. We need to remember the gift of our talents, as well as the experiences we have the opportunity to live every day.

Gratitude for all things shows as we move through our daily lives and touch others with our own individual magic.

We are what we attract. What we put out into the world in thoughts, actions and deeds will show who we really are … how our abundance plays out in our world. If we do not feel abundant, what is missing from life to make this so? I believe this can be changed so easily by changing the perspective of how we see and feel life.

I ask you how creatively responsible you are?

Do you help to make your world safer, healthier, wiser, richer and a much better place to raise your family?

Instead of feeling alone and overwhelmed by family dilemmas, we begin to connect with other parents, children, youth and seniors by extending our families outwards.

Family are not only the people who have our blood ... they can also be the people who make up our life tapestry to help us to be the best we can be.

We can all feel the comfort, help, pleasure and tangible support from those surrounding us.

Do you know how abundantly gifted you are?

Do you share your precious gifts, which are something we often take for granted, with the new connections and relationships created daily? As we cross the lines drawn between youth and adulthood, acknowledging both our seniors and the youth, the frail and the able, are you a competent community leader?

Are you aware of how abundantly financial you are and that money is just energy and has no limits? To support your community usually costs little to nothing, and yet, our community can become some of the treasures of our lives. You can't buy more safety, health, wisdom or wealth, but together we can all create them. We need to feel less burdened financially and less dependent on outside institutions and government. We all can find the 'citizens way'.

Having been born and bred in the country, I was always aware of the importance of community and how dependent we were on our neighbours and friends. If you want to create a better future, find a new kind of trust. Allow your neighbours to become people you can count on and allow them to count on you. Through this, a profound sense of security will begin to emerge.

Most people are not aware of just how powerful they are. Are you?

We find our own way, and that sense of power leads us to hold celebrations, acclaiming our successes, while recognising our frailties and those among us who have passed away. Be grateful for your power and the abundance it can bring to your life.

Has your day today been amazing? Has something happened that you will remember in the future? It could be something to do with your work, a friend does something special, or you are told 'I love you'.

We tend to take so much for granted and many times are not aware of how blessed and abundant we really are.

Living in flow, fulfilling our destiny and being on purpose by acknowledging the abundance in the gifts we ourselves have, are part of who we are whilst manifesting this flow as we go about our daily lives.

Be who you are … show the world who you are by contributing to the lives of those around you, who you not only love, but those who are here to give you the lessons in life to help you become the magnificent being that you are.

Is your heart singing?

I believe, we are all Awesomely Abundant!

ABOUT THE AUTHOR

Jennie Gorman is a mother, grandmother and down to earth business women who lives and loves life with a passion for people.

Living this passion daily she aspires to support others to do the same to realise their own dreams.

Jennie's focus is all about the WHY of life for herself and her clients. Her key question is always - Why are you here and what is your purpose? Over many years of learning and teaching about relationships she has recognised that there is no difference between who you are in your personal and business life. It is all about being authentic – **your REAL self**.

Known as 'the people connector', her passion is helping entrepreneurs catapult their business into the 21st century by utilising what she calls the 'New Business' style of marketing and other smart business growth strategies, such as masterminding, social media, networking, and outsourcing!

She says, **"It is all about authenticity ... trust and integrity will take you wherever you want to go in business, if you are REAL."**

Jennie helps make people's dreams come into reality. In 2009 she developed a MasterMinding formula and has proof that it works! This formula has a solid platform. It is also a growing organism that expands monthly as she learns, develops and experiences more by adding new skills, contacts and experts to the team.

She knows this process also helps support SMEs to create business relationships so they can claim their place in the marketplace, thus gaining the necessary and appropriate skills via masterminding and networking.

She helps motivate and inspire people to perform at a level that they hadn't yet recognised through personal mentoring and MasterMind groups.

As a supporter of entrepreneurs, solo and SME professionals, her aim is to teach the art of successful business relationships. She does this by educating her clients to develop greater skills for long lasting results by relationship marketing, networking, communicating, social media and referral based business strategies.

Her long-term success lies within her extraordinary network of people that offer skills, talent and resources. Her unique and natural gift is to bring people together to create the perfect fit and ultimately change people's lives through relationship building and trusted communication.

In 1989, Jennie commenced her first business, 'My Connexions' as a promoter, and in 1992 she started a Personal Development and Natural Therapies Centre, which was the start to the work she continues today.

In 1995 Connexions Unlimited was born and Jennie moved to business education, promoting national and international speakers and trainers, as well as creating her own events educating how to build relationships. In 2009 she incorporated into the Connexions Unlimited structure her own formula of Business MasterMind Groups, which has proven to be her passion

MasterMinding gives Jennie a way of supporting people, especially entrepreneurs, in all business skill sets. She believes that group synergy is paramount in creating suitable advisory boards, who keep each other accountable and real, so their businesses grow and participants reach their individual goals.

Jennie believes that this can happen by relationship building. Teaching clients to understand their individual wealth profile, and using networking and then masterminding, to find their niche market to increase their profits and grow their business.

Motivating and inspiring people to perform at a level that they hadn't yet recognised is paramount to Jennie. She educates via ongoing mentoring, masterminding, workshops, speaking engagements, networking and specialist events. Being part of her MasterMind Groups is the positive add-on to go to the next level.

Her specialties are helping her clients to:
- create their circle of influence
- stay accountable
- create an advisory board
- build a support network
- find their niche market
- understand the importance of authenticity.

Working with start-up business people has taken Jennie's business to another level. She does this by giving talks,

AWESOME AUTHENTICITY

workshops and mentoring those whom she feels need the extra support to guide them and their new businesses through the starting gate to success! For her, this is her 'pay it forward' strategy for which she has a great passion, understanding what it is like not to have the practical and honest support when you first commence in business.

Jennie knows that trust, integrity, authenticity and sincerity are fundamental to maintaining fulfilling, purposeful and satisfying relationships in both personal and business life.

She asks you 'What is it to be awesome?'

For her, it is being real, accountable and responsible, to not only self, but to others too.

Jennie believes that ethical business practices are the proof of authenticity.

"Transferring your passion to your business is far easier than working a job that is like a knife in your gut every day."

AWESOME AUTHENTICITY

www.awesomeauthenticity.com.au
www.connexionsunlimited.com.au
www.businessmastermindgroups.com.au
www.facebook.com/JennieGormanThePeopleConnector
https://www.facebook.com/jennie.gorman
http://au.linkedin.com/in/jenniegorman

jennie@awesomeauthenticity.com.au
P O Box 118, Clayfield, Queensland, Australia

www.ingramcontent.com/pod-product-compliance
Lightning Source LLC
Chambersburg PA
CBHW070647160426
43194CB00009B/1610